KNOW HOW KNOW WHY

BIRDS

Written by Keith and Jonathan West

Illustrations by Mike Atkinson

www.rourkepublishing.com

Library of Congress Cataloging-in-Publication Data

West, Keith and Jonathan -
   Birds / Keith and Jonathan West.
       p. cm. -- (Know How, Know Why)
   Includes Bibliographical references and index
   ISBN 1-60044-258-7 (hardcover)
   ISBN 978-1-60044-346-6 (paperback)

Printed in the USA

CG/CG

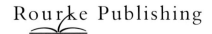

Rourke Publishing

www.rourkepublishing.com – sales@rourkepublishing.com
Post Office Box 3328, Vero Beach, FL 32964

SWIFTS, SWALLOWS, AND MARTINS

Swifts, swallows, and martins are summer visitors, simply "passing through" on their long journeys to other parts of the world. The three birds are beautiful to watch in flight, and their elegant silhouette against a summer sky is distinctive.

How can I tell swifts, swallows, and martins apart ?

A swift.

A swallow.

A house martin.

Despite looking similar at first glance, these birds have several distinguishing features. Swifts have blackish plumage with upper parts that can appear metallic blue, and pale chins and throats. Swallows are slimmer, with unusually long tail streamers and have red chins and foreheads. House martins' tails are only slightly forked, with no tail streamers.

What is migration ?

When it gets cold and there is little to eat, many species of bird will set off on long journeys of hundreds of miles. Some head north to the Arctic Circle, where the long hours of daylight lead to a flowering of life. Swifts, swallows, and martins mainly head to warmer climes, such as Africa. Common swift leave Europe in August, head to Africa and return in April, where they settle to breed.

A swallow skims the fields for insects.

What are the features of swifts ?

Swifts have sickle-shaped wings which taper out at each end. This shape allows for faster, more agile flight than that of the swallow. When flying, swifts use short wing beats followed by longer wing glides. One wing beats faster than another which acts as a rudder to balance their long wings —their stumpy tails are too short to do this alone.

Swifts are agile fliers.

FACT BYTES

Swifts once nested in cliffs but have adapted to live near humans.

Young swallows return to the same area where they were born to make their nests.

Where do these birds nest ?

Swallows nest inside stables and barns and form cup-shaped nests. House martins nest outside houses—usually under eaves (the overhanging parts of roofs give birds plenty of space to get under), and form compact nests made from mud. When they leave their nests they rarely rest, spending most of their time "on the wing."

House martins nest underneath eaves of buildings.

What do they eat ?

Swifts, swallows, and house martins all eat small flying insects—including flies, aphids and beetles. Swifts and house martins fly high into the sky to catch them, whereas swallows fly low over fields and rivers. Swifts have great "catching" mechanisms—they have tiny bills which they use as funnels to draw insects in. They then store the insects in their throat pouch until they have collected enough to feed their young.

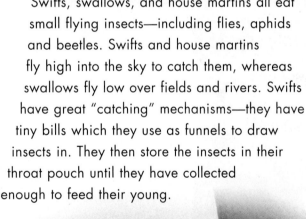

A swift spends almost all its adult life on the wing.

SWIFTS, SWALLOWS, AND MARTINS

DOVES, CUCKOOS, AND PIGEONS

Doves and pigeons are often kept in captivity. They have quite plump bodies and smallish heads. They are powerful fliers and their wings make loud noises during takeoff. Cuckoos can be heard in spring and summer but are rarely seen.

Where do pigeons come from ❓

Tame pigeons are descendants of rock doves, large birds that lived in the wild in Africa, Asia, Europe, and the Middle East. They arrived in North America when northern Europeans emigrated to Nova Scotia, Canada, in the early 1600s. Some people, especially those in cities and towns, started to domesticate rock doves. Rock doves still exist in the wild, and their domesticated brothers are known as "feral" pigeons —the familiar gray birds we have come to associate with wide public spaces in towns and cities.

Why have pigeons got a bad press ❓

As the feral pigeon population increases there are more pigeon droppings, which cause damage to buildings and can land on people's heads! The birds are also considered dirty—however, you can often see them taking baths in public fountains. Like any animal, their droppings can harbor germs, so always wash your hands if you ever touch them.

What's the difference between pigeons and doves ❓

A collared dove.

Not much! Doves are a type of pigeon. Many people think doves are smaller, but this isn't always the case. The word "pigeon" comes from the French word "pijon" meaning a "winged rat." They are not particularly attractive and feral pigeons have dull plumage. White doves, however, are considered beautiful and are associated with peace, joy, and romance!

FACT BYTES

Cuckoos are actually very fussy birds, who choose the "host" nest for their eggs very carefully. Different "gentes" (or races) of cuckoo choose the nests of different birds, including those of robins and redstarts.

Why do people race pigeons

Pigeons have good homing instincts and can find their way back to their lofts from great distances. Betting on which pigeon will get home first has developed into a serious sport with around eighty thousand fanciers (pigeon breeders) raising about two million birds a year. Some pigeons race for up to 500 miles (800 km) a day!

Why do cuckoos not build nests

Some species of cuckoo are known as parasitic, which means that they don't actually rear their own young, but palm them off to other adult birds! A cuckoo places her own egg into the nest of other birds who then raise the youngster as their own.

Feral pigeons are a familiar sight in towns and cities.

How do baby cuckoos survive in "foreign" nests

If "hosts" are fooled into believing the eggs are theirs, they'll sit on them until the baby cuckoos hatch. The babies have scoop-like depressions on their necks, and will instinctively push anything they touch out of the nest. This means that other babies and eggs may fall out. When this happens, the host mothers may decide to devote their energies to looking after the cuckoos! The cuckoos grow very quickly and will often be larger than their adopted parents.

DOVES, CUCKOOS, AND PIGEONS

CROWS

Rooks often gather in flocks and are seen in empty fields in winter. Crows are only seen alone or in pairs. Jays are members of the crow family and they are very colorful.

Where would I see rooks ❓

Rooks are now quite rare. In recent years, farmers have sprayed pesticide on their crops to control the threat of creepy-crawlies called wireworms. Rooks, feeding on seedlings, were poisoned and so total population numbers soon declined. However, some are still seen hunting for worms in the furrows of muddy fields.

How can I tell which member of the family I've seen ❓

The carrion (common) crow and rook are the two most easily confused as both are large, dark birds. However, carrion crows don't have baggy "trousers" around their legs, nor the fluffy foreheads of rooks. They have shorter, deeper bills, broader wings and are slower in flight. If you see birds that look like bits of both, they are likely to be hooded crows which have light gray backs.

What do magpies eat ❓

Magpies are large, black and white birds with long tails. They have attractive, glossy black feathers that take on a metallic dark blue or green sheen. When in flight, they are easy to spot as their black and white wings are in full view. They have a reputation for being greedy thieves which is well earned. There is very little that they won't eat, or steal, given the chance.

A hooded crow.

Where do crows make their homes

The carrion crow is found in England, Wales, and Scotland. The hooded crow is found in Scotland, Iceland, Europe, and Asia. You will notice from the map that, whilst appearing commonly across Europe, crows are rare in Ireland where few breeding records exist.

A carrion crow.

Where can I find a jay

The common jay can be seen in woodland, parks and suburbs across North Africa, Asia, and Europe. Jays are colorful crows with mostly brownish-pink features. They are very sociable and can imitate the calls of many other birds. Jays build their untidy looking nests in trees and shrubs. They are shy woodland birds, rarely moving far from cover. Their screaming calls usually let you know that they are about.

FACT BYTES

Jays are egg thieves which also kill and eat young birds. Although they look attractive, gardeners hate them as they eat soft fruit.

The common jay can be found in woodland parks and suburbs.

CROWS

CREEPERS AND NUTHATCHES

As members of the bird order *Passeriformes*, these passerines are characteristically "perching" birds with strong voices!

What is the coolest thing about nuthatches ?

Most nuthatches are woodland birds. They get their name from the Eurasian nuthatches, which wedge nuts in crevices of trees and then hack away at them with their strong beaks. Unlike woodpeckers, which can only run up trees, nuthatches have an amazing ability to run downward, very fast, without falling off! They have big heads, short tails, powerful bills, and strong feet. They often climb underneath branches with their heads facing the ground.

How easy are they to spot ?

You'll have to be sharp-eyed! For a start, nuthatches are relatively small birds. White-breasted nuthatches, for example, are only 5 in. (14 cm) long. Pygmy nuthatches are found mainly in the United States and are around 3.5 in. (9 cm) long, whilst their Eurasian equivalents, brown-headed nuthatches, are only 4 in. (10 cm) in length. They creep up trees so fast and in so many different directions that they can be very difficult to spot!

How many types of tree creeper are there ?

There are two types of tree creeper—tree creepers and short-toed tree creepers. The easiest way to tell the difference between the two is by listening to their song. Tree creepers have different voices to their short-toed cousins. Their calls are a repeated "sree." Short-toed treecreepers make loud "teet-teet-teet" sounds.

What are the holes we see in tree trunks

These could well be home to tree creepers. These clever little birds will hack away at the soft, fibrous bark of trees, such as the coast redwood, to hollow out their homes. Inside, they are well protected from the wind and rain. To get food, tree creepers make their way up the trunks, and then the branches of trees in spiral actions, occasionally stopping to retrieve insects from the crevices in the bark.

Where are wall creepers found

Wall creepers are often thought of as part of the nuthatch family but could be considered a species of their own. They are small birds, living in the high mountains of southern Eurasia, in the Pyrenean and Alpine mountain ranges. They can "creep" up rock faces and breed on steep cliffs, deep ravines and gorges with waterfalls.

A tree creeper collects insects for her nestlings.

FACT BYTES

Algerian nuthatches were not discovered until 1975. There are about 150 known pairs alive today.

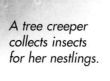

WARBLERS

Like wall creepers and nuthatches, warblers are also passerine birds. Some types are very rare indeed. Dartford warblers are one of the rarest birds in Britain.

What types of warblers are there ❓

A painted redstart.

A wood warbler.

There are two types of warbler, Old World and New World. Old World warblers grow up to 10 in. (25 cm) long and like to feed on berries and insects. New World warblers include the Nashville Warbler and blue-winged warbler.

Where do warblers live ❓

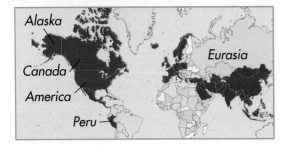

Alaska

Canada

America

Peru

Eurasia

Although New World warblers can be seen in Eurasia and America, their real homes are in hotter places where they spend two-thirds of their time. Blackpoll warblers migrate incredible distances,

spending winter in Peru and having a summer nesting period in Alaska and Canada. During spring migration, they average about 30 miles (50 km) a day before making landfall in Canada.

Why are warblers loved so much by enthusiasts ❓

In addition to their beautiful songs, warblers are amongst the most attractive of all birds. Aquatic warblers are small, slim birds with sandy colored plumage streaked with lines. They have beautiful sandy colored crowns and rather spiky looking tails. Attractive but unobtrusive, wood warblers have bright yellow upper parts, throats and upper chests, and white under parts. These warblers are widespread and numerous in deciduous forests in Europe and reach their highest densities in Wales, UK.

What is the "warble"

This is the name for the song created by any one member of the warbler family, although it can vary considerably from one bird to another. Old World warblers may have very sweet songs, whereas some New World Warblers make noises that are squeaky and "buzzy." Northern parula warblers have songs that can be compared to a finger being run up a comb! Some people claim to be able to tell the species of a bird by its song. Warblers are very shy birds.

The whitethroat can be seen more commonly in bushes and thickets on the field margins.

How do warblers catch their food

Warblers are insect eaters and this explains their frenzied activity. They can catch insects on the wing, but also look for food hidden in the crevices of trees. They like to eat aphids, which they cunningly extract from the underside of a leaf. Most warblers look for food above ground level, finding insects with their short, pointed beaks.

A willow warbler.

FACT BYTES

Dartford warblers can appear as if they are on fire as they have reddish looks. They do not like harsh winters and die in extreme cold. Some can eat eighty percent of their body weight in insects every day! They are, therefore, essential in the control of insects.

WARBLERS

DIPPERS

Dippers are any of five species of songbirds, found in western North America, South America, Europe, and Asia. All live near water and the amazing thing about dippers is that they're the only songbirds that can swim and dive. Enlarged preen glands for waterproofing the feathers, dense plumage and highly developed nictitating (blinking) membranes to protect the eyes are adaptations to their aquatic habits.

How can I spot a dipper **?**

Dippers have strong legs and short, square tipped tails. Usually about 7 in. (18 cm) long, their throats and breasts are dirty shades of white. Unusually for water birds, they have no webs on their feet and show little else to make them suitable for an aquatic life other than membranes to protect their eyes and movable flaps to close their nostrils under water.

What is a dipper's song like **?**

A dipper's songs are like a series of chattering whistles. Their flight call sounds like "srit" or "tsit." Sometimes the calls are harsher "tser" sounds. Dippers can copy the songs of other birds and mix them with their own.

Where are dippers found **?**

They can be spotted diving into water to find food and nesting on cliffs, boulders and stream banks of clear, rocky creeks and rivers. In winter, they often move to streams and rivers at lower elevations and concentrate in higher numbers, sometimes using very narrow creeks and slower-moving rivers or lakes.

FACT BYTES

Dippers swim with their wings open.

Dippers often swim underwater. They can even walk on the bottom of a river bed as they search for food.

How common are dippers

Although the dipper population is stable, they have declined, or disappeared, from certain streams that have become polluted. It has been suggested that nest dippers are indicaters of good quality water because they need a plentiful supply of aquatic insects and fish to feed their young.

Dippers are often seen amongst rocks along the water's edge, bobbing in and out of the water.

What do dippers eat

Dippers feed on aquatic insects, such as flies, larvae and worms, that they collect by swimming in mountain streams and searching around under the stones of the stream bed. They often disappear underwater whilst gathering food. They also eat fish eggs and very small fish fry.

Adult dippers have a brown head and neck. Their rump, wings and tail are very dark whilst their chin, throat and breast parts are bright white. They have a distinctive chestnut patch on their underside.

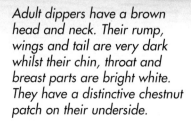

WAGTAILS, PIPITS, AND LARKS

Wagtails and pipits come from the same family: *Motacillidae*. There are 26 species and subspecies that live across the wide area of Europe, Asia, and North America. They are difficult to tell apart!

What do these birds have in common

Wagtails are black and white in color whilst pipits generally have dull plumage, with mixtures of black and white or brown feathers for camouflage. They are insect eaters, with slender bills to reach inside crevices. They tend to live in the open countryside, and sing "on the wing." The most distinctive characteristic of both wagtails and pipits is their long tail.

Why do they wag their tails

There is no definite answer to this question. Many believe that wagtails and pipits need their long, thin tails to act as balancing mechanisms (rather like the way humans hold out their arms when trying to balance) to prevent them falling over when chasing flies! Visit golf courses, and other open areas, in the summer where you should see pied wagtails.

What do wagtails' eggs look like

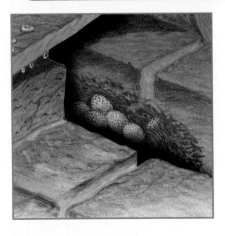

The eggs are smooth and glossy. They are usually in clutches of 4-6 eggs and are laid in cup-like nests made of plant material such as weeds and grass. The nests are found near water, but are usually well hidden on the ground, hidden under clumps of grass.

A pied wagtail.

Which pipits am I most likely to see

A rock pipit.

A meadow pipit.

A golden pipit.

Some meadow pipits migrate to Northern Africa, but in the summer months they are widespread from Greenland to central Asia. They run and walk on open moors, revealing a brown and white streaky breast. Rock pipits can be found breeding on the coasts of Britain, Scandinavia, and Russia. They have dark brown plumage on their top feathers to act as camouflage against rocks, and are buff underneath. If you head for exotic climes you might see the stunning golden pipits, with their bright yellow undersides. They do not migrate, living full-time in eastern Africa.

What are larks

Larks are similar in coloring to pipits. Skylarks, found across Eurasia and northern Africa, have streaked brown and white plumage. However, these birds walk upright, rather than hopping along like pipits, and are famous for their glorious airborne songs. Shore larks (right), which breed in Eurasia and North and South America, have horn-like feathers on their heads which they can raise at will.

FACT BYTES

Although skylarks can be easily overlooked when on the ground, their distinctive song flight makes them more visible as they fly vertically into the air.

WAGTAILS, PIPITS, AND LARKS

PENGUINS, PELICANS, AND AUKS

These birds are adapted for surviving life in colder climates. Penguins spend most of their time in water. Pelicans are the only birds with webbing between all four toes. Auks dive underwater for food.

How do penguins get around

Penguins are often thought of as birds that struggle to walk on ice and snow. Sometimes they drop to their bellies, and push themselves along using their flippers. Most penguins have very short legs and large, fleshy pads for feet to help them waddle.

Where do penguins live

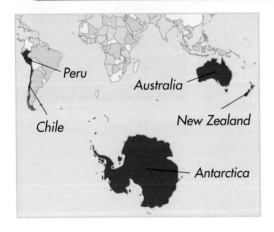

Peru

Australia

Chile

New Zealand

Antarctica

The largest penguins, emperor penguins, are found on Antarctic coasts. As are adelie penguins, which hunt for krill (similar to fish). Little penguins, which are 16 in. (40 cm) tall, breed on the coasts and islands of south and southeast Australia and New Zealand, while humboldt penguins make nests in caves or burrows on the coastlines of Peru and Chile.

How do pelicans get their food

Most pelicans can take fish from the surface of the water, but their trusted technique is "plunge diving." After spotting a shoal of fish, sometimes from a height of 40 ft (12 m), they'll dive straight into the water where they will scoop up fish and water with their massive bills. They can then drain the water by lifting their heads. To spot this kind of activity in the brown pelican, you'd need to visit the Pacific coasts of the Americas or the Atlantic coast from northern USA to Brazil.

Who are the members of the auk family

Auks come from the family *alcidae* and look similar to penguins, but aren't related at all. They have little wings, which means they can fly—but not very well! They excel at diving and swimming. The auk family includes little auks, dumpy, 8.5 in. (22 cm) tall seabirds which spend their winters in the North Atlantic Ocean. Razorbills are larger, standing at 17 in. (43 cm), and have distinctive white stripes on their bills. Everyone knows the comical-looking puffin (right). When finding food for their young, they dive underwater and pack eels crossways in their bills.

A puffin.

A pelican diving for fish.

Why did great auks become extinct

At 30 in. (75 cm) in height, great auks were the biggest auks ever. Although excellent swimmers, great auks couldn't fly which made them very vulnerable to humans. Records show that they were hunted for food in the eighth century. Many great auks lived in Canada, Greenland, Iceland, Scotland, and Norway but became an officially extinct species when the last pair was killed in July 1844.

Great auks were hunted to extinction in 1844.

FACT BYTES

The largest penguins, emperor penguins, weigh 60 lb (27.41 kg). Fairy penguins are the smallest. They weigh just 2.2 lb (1 kg).

STORKS AND IBISES

Storks and ibises are large birds with plump bodies and long legs, necks, and bills. Their long legs help them to wade in shallow water, where they feed on fish, snails, crabs, and amphibians. Unusually for aquatic creatures, their toes are not webbed. These birds are found in freshwater habitats across Europe, mostly in warm regions free from freezing winter conditions.

Why are storks rare ?

Europe

White storks, which are seen in Europe, have had many of their breeding areas destroyed. They like swampy areas, which have now been drained. Black storks like old forests—many of these forests have been chopped down.

What do storks eat ?

Storks feed in drier areas than most birds in their order and enjoy eating frogs, snakes, mice, insects, and baby birds. European white storks feed primarily in shallow water and grassland, but also at the edges of crop fields. Marabou storks often behave more like vultures. They soar high up in search of food.

Why are their bills so long ?

Long bills are useful tools for pulling creatures from water or mud. Ibises have long, thin, downcurving bills. Storks' bills are long and straight but often curve up, or down, at the tip.

A European white stork.

What do bald ibises look like

Bald ibises (right) have no hair on their heads. Their plumage is black with metallic green and purple-brown gloss. The feathers around their necks droop like poorly kept manes. Their beaks are generally red. Once widespread throughout southern

Europe, North Africa, and West Asia, bald ibises are now extremely rare. They nest in colonies on steep cliffs, where their young are relatively safe from attack.

What are the closest relatives to ibises

Spoonbills, which are found in some areas of southern England, are the closest relative to ibises. Large, mainly white birds with black legs, their most distinctive feature is their huge spoon-like bills with hooked tips. Spoonbills use their bill for searching out food—fish, frogs, snakes, molluscs, and carrion—in the mud of marshlands.

A spoon-like bill gives the spoonbill their name.

FACT BYTES

Have you wondered why storks don't eat toads? After all, they eat frogs. The answer is that toads, when picked up, squirt poisons from their bodies.

Bald ibises were once quite common in some parts of the world. They became extinct in Turkey in 1984.

STORKS AND IBISES

GULLS AND TERNS

Gulls are well-known seabirds. Sixteen species are very common and they often live near humans. Gulls breed near coasts, marshes, or lakes. Some types are now common inland—they can be seen in fields following tractors and also on rubbish dumps. Terns are also seabirds but they are smaller than gulls. Their wings are pointed and narrow and they have long, pointed bills and forked tails.

How is it possible to tell the age of a gull ?

You can tell the age of some smaller gull species, from their first to their fourth years, when they moult. During their first year, common gulls have plain mid-wing panels. Their wing tips are dusty brown and gray in color, becoming darker gray near their body. The inner wings are coarsely marked. By the second year, the gulls' underbodies are white, their bodies are gray and their wing tips are black with small white markings. The wing tips of adult birds are less dark and their markings consist of large white patches.

A juvenile gull.

Do laughing gulls really laugh ?

Laughing gulls make calls that sound like a loud and crazy human laugh. Their call is fairly high pitched and sounds a bit like "haaa-hee-hee-hee-ha." They live in colonies that can consist of thousands of nests and are scavengers, that are known to take food directly out of the beaks of other birds!

A laughing gull.

FACT BYTES

Arctic terns have the longest migration of all birds.

Lesser crested terns (right) often share their nesting sites with other types of tern, or with gulls.

Do herring gulls eat herrings

They do eat herrings—but they like other food too. They eat scraps thrown from boats, small birds, eggs, and small fish. Before and after the breeding season, herring gulls appear in large flocks in harbors where they scavenge for scraps from fishing boats. These gulls nest on islands and on cliffs, often in large colonies. The chicks scatter from the nesting areas a day after hatching, hiding in clumps of grass, awaiting feeding.

Why do gulls follow boats

They want the food they know will be thrown from boats. You might be able to recognize seabirds called manx shearwaters by their flight as they follow boats. They flap their wings quickly at intervals, and then glide, or 'shear' over the waves. They tip their wings to the right and then to the left as they ride on the "updraughts" of the waves.

An Arctic Tern.

Gulls following a trawler.

Do Arctic terns spend all of their life in the Arctic

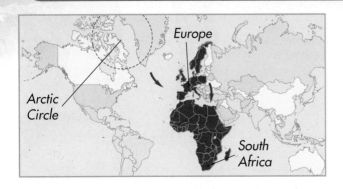

No. Arctic terns can also be seen in northern Europe. In winter, they migrate to South Africa. About 15 in. (38 cm) in length, they are smaller than common terns and can be recognized by their blood-red bills. Arctic terns' lower throats, breasts and bellies are gray and their upper throats are white. Their wings are gray and their short legs are a reddish color.

HERONS, EGRETS, AND FLAMINGOS

There are many types of egrets and most are white in color. Although there are many types of bittern, they are elusive and difficult to study. Flamingos are found in parts of South America, Africa, and parts of Asia and in southern France and Spain. Herons are large, distinctive birds and easily recognized.

What is the difference between the great and little egret

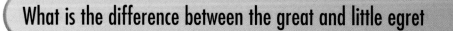

A great egret.

A little egret.

Great egrets are 40 in. (100 cm) in height whereas little egrets stand at just 25 in. (65 cm). Little egrets are white with black legs and have bright yellow toes while great egrets have brown legs and toes. Great egrets have slower, more dignified wingbeats than little egrets, and also have the longer legs and necks of the two.

How can I tell bitterns from gray herons ?

Bitterns are buff brown and slightly smaller than herons. They have stocky shapes and their thick necks are usually hunched into their shoulders. In flight, the wingbeats are much quicker than herons'. Their coloring looks owl-like in flight. Gray herons have long necks. The two birds actually look quite different and should not be confused.

What do bitterns and herons eat ?

Bitterns will eat fish, frogs, newts, tadpoles, leeches, worms, and any insects that live in the water. They like to live and feed near swamps, marshes and reed beds. Gray herons eat small fish, tadpoles, frogs, reptiles, insects, and even small birds. They live and eat near overgrown rivers, ponds, lakes, swamps, and woodlands near water.

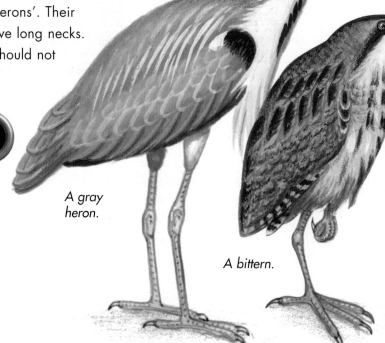

A gray heron.

A bittern.

How do gray herons catch their food

Gray herons wait patiently at river banks for fish. They often stand for hours. As soon as fish swim by, they move! They use their long, angled neck to dart forward in a flash, pouncing on their prey. You are more likely to see the familiar sight of hunched herons waiting to feed than herons in flight. They stretch their huge wings and fly with slow, measured beats.

A young flamingo takes its first tentative steps after hatching.

What do baby flamingos look like

Flamingo chicks look like geese when they are first hatched. Flamingos incubate their eggs for a period of thirty days, with both the male and female swapping shifts to sit on a single egg. During the hatching process, adult flamingos will try to help the chick push its way out of the shell. Young flamingos are not pink but dull brown in color.

Why are flamingos pink

Flamingos are often more white than pink. The legs and beak are pink. Young flamingos are not pink but dull brown in color. It is the coloring in the food that they eat that turns them pink. They tend to eat small creatures such as shrimp that live in the water, and plankton.

FACT BYTES

Flamingos only lay one egg. Flamingo chicks have no baby brothers or sisters to grow up with.

Most baby birds have their mouths open wide when the mother returns to the nest. This tells her that her chicks want to be fed.

The striking plumage of a flamingo.

ALBATROSSES

There are many varieties of albatross—birds that often follows ships out at sea. While people think of them as large birds, some of them are, in fact, quite small.

Where would I find albatrosses ?

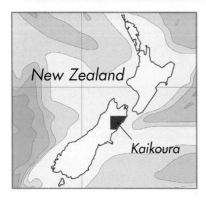

New Zealand

Kaikoura

Probably the best place to go to spot albatrosses is New Zealand. In an area of the country called Kaikoura you can find five varieties of great albatross. There are also eight varieties of smaller albatross in New Zealand. Other places to look for albatrosses are South America, South Africa, and Australia.

What do European albatrosses look like ?

Black browed albatrosses are the species most likely to be seen in Europe. They sometimes visit in summer and fall. On a few occasions, brown albatrosses have been spotted amongst gannet coastal colonies in Scotland. Large birds, they can be up to 37 in. (95 cm) in length. Their wingspans are about the size of the mute swans'. Their underwings are white with broad, black edgings. Albatrosses have short, dark eyestrips and their bills are yellow with distinctive yellow tips.

Snowy albatrosses soaring in the sky.

What can harm albatrosses ?

Thousands are killed every year by longline fishing. In longline fishing, long lengths of line covered in baited hooks are thrown out of fishing boats. Fish are caught on the hooks, but the hooks also snare albatrosses. Sometimes albatrosses can harm their own kind. They can fight over carrion, such as beached whales. They can also fight over smaller dead birds.

Are albatrosses rare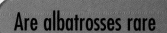

Some are. While snowy albatrosses are relatively common in New Zealand where there are about 32,000 breeding pairs, very few are found elsewhere in the world. Wandering albatrosses are very rarely seen in Europe. One was spotted in France in 1830, in Belgium in 1833, in Italy in 1957 and, most recently, in Portugal in 1963.

Do albatrosses live a long time ?

Some do. Buller's albatrosses can live up to fifty years. One great albatross became known as grandma. She lived to be 61 years old. Endemic breeders in New Zealand, northern royal albatrosses are traditionally eaten by Maoris.

Maoris, New Zealand's native inhabitants.

FACT BYTES

Albatrosses are the world's largest flying birds. Their wing spans are 11 ft (3.4 m) and they can weigh up to 14 lb (6.5 kg).

Who was the ancient mariner ?

The poet Samuel Taylor Coleridge wrote a poem called *The Rime of the Ancient Mariner*. The mariner was cursed because he had killed an albatross following his ship. He had to wander Earth warning people about the curse of killing innocent birds. Perhaps Coleridge got his idea from the wandering albatross.

WADERS

Members of one of the larger bird families, waders are common on coasts and seen throughout most of the world. They tend to have long, thin bills to pick invertebrates from the soil or mud and live near water, along shores and marshes. Plovers and oystercatchers are both waders.

Why do oystercatchers have blunt-tipped bills

Their bills are adapted for hammering and opening cockles and mussels—oystercatchers' food. The tips of their bills are slightly flattened, which makes them look a little like knives. Oystercatchers feed on tidal flats or fields near the sea. They can be seen running about in groups on mudflats and sandy beaches as they search for things to eat.

Where do oystercatchers nest

Oystercatchers usually make their nests on the ground, on sandy or rocky areas. They may line the inside with shells and shell fragments. The eggs are smooth, glossy and grayish-yellow with bold markings. Most oystercatchers lay eggs in clutches of three. The chicks are unmistakable as they are long-legged with slender bills.

Oystercatcher eggs lie in slight depressions on the ground.

Where can plovers be found

Little ringed plovers are summer visitors to Europe and are slightly smaller than ringed plovers. Like most plovers, they live near fresh water with shallow muddy margins and rich food supplies. Semi-palmated plovers are North American birds but have been seen in Britain and Spain on a few occasions. In winter, it is possible to spot killdeers (left), which are North American plovers.

How do waders look after their young ❓

Many wader chicks are looked after by both parents. However, sometimes the females leave their young before they are fledged. The males stay until the chicks are ready to fly. As most waders will migrate long distances, it is important that they learn to fly well so that they will survive the long trips.

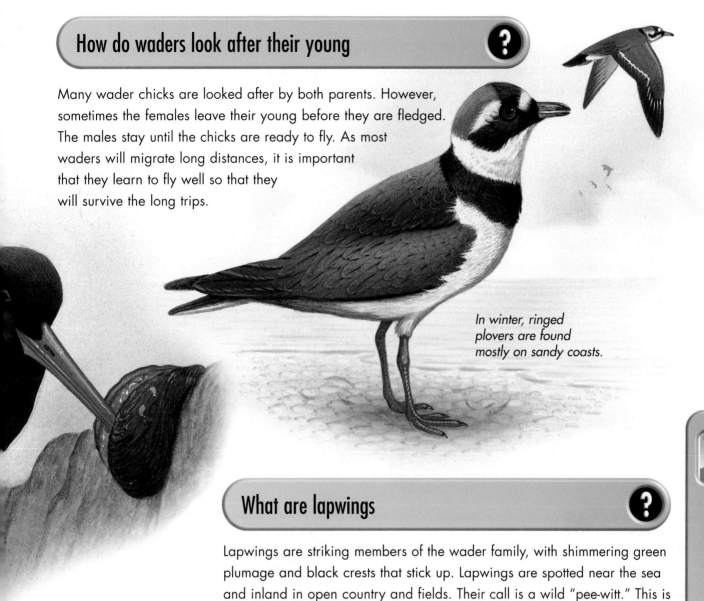

In winter, ringed plovers are found mostly on sandy coasts.

An oystercatcher's bill is adapted for opening mussels.

What are lapwings ❓

Lapwings are striking members of the wader family, with shimmering green plumage and black crests that stick up. Lapwings are spotted near the sea and inland in open country and fields. Their call is a wild "pee-witt." This is usually heard during the nesting season when the male flies over the nesting area. The nests themselves are hollows, scraped out by the lapwing's feet, and shaped by the pressure of their bodies sitting on them.

FACT BYTES

With pied plumage and long, red bills oystercatchers are very striking shorebirds. Oystercatchers walk about in groups with heads bowed and bills pointed downwards.

Thousands of waders rest in Ireland for a short while before going to or coming back from their winter stay in Africa.

A lapwing on its nest.

GANNETS AND BOOBIES

Gannets are large sea birds with long, pointed wings and tails. Their bills are straight and pointed. They can be seen diving for fish, often from great heights. There are different types of booby. Smaller than gannets, they can only be found in the southern hemisphere.

How do gannets look after their eggs ❓

Cape gannets' parents are both involved in the incubation process which lasts for 42-46 days until hatching. Gannets use their foot webs which are richly irrigated with blood vessels to incubate the eggs. The structure of the foot webs makes sure that the eggs stay warm. Gannets' eggs have an uneven white appearance with unusual blue layers under the surface shells.

Where do gannets lay their eggs ❓

Gannets nest in groups, called colonies, on steep rocks and cliffs along the coast or on undisturbed islands. Their nests are usually a bill-stab apart! Cape gannets use dried droppings (guano), feathers, bones, and other debris to build their nests.

Gannets dive from a great height, folding back their wings just before they enter the water.

FACT BYTES

Booby is the old Spanish word for clown. Boobies got their names from sailors who saw their tameness as a sign of stupidity and they are also considered to have stupid looks on their faces!

Gannets and boobies fish by diving on their prey from great heights. They follow and chase their prey through the water. They can drop vertically into the sea from heights as great as 150 ft (45 m).

How do I recognize gannets

Young gannets have gray-brown plumage. If you look closely at young gannets you will see that their plumage seems to be covered with a beautiful silver sheen. Adult gannets are white with yellow heads. They can be seen feeding in flocks. Strong flyers, they alternate between flapping and gliding. and often fly in groups.

Where will I find brown and blue-footed boobies

Brown boobies live and breed in tropical waters near the coast. They also breed on some islands near the Red Sea. Blue-footed boobies are found along the South American coast. At first glance, you'll wonder why they are so named because their bright turquoise-blue, webbed feet are covered in dark brown and white plumage.

A blue-footed booby.

What happens when boobies' chicks hatch

Chicks become noisy before they even break from their shells. These are the signals for the parents to prepare for hatching and switch from incubation (when the egg is under the foot webs) to brooding (when the egg is placed on top of the feet webs). The young are looked after for about thirteen weeks before being forced to fly out to sea.

How do gannets and boobies float

Air sacs situated just under the skin.

Gannets and boobies have air sacs under their skins. This gives them buoyancy in the water. They also have water-repellent plumage, and their bones contain relatively large volumes of air space to aid buoyancy.

OSTRICHES, EMUS, AND RHEAS

Members of the ratite family, these birds are large and unable to fly. Ostriches, emus, and rheas are some of the larger members of this family with features in common— all have strong legs which help them to run, and massive claws on their feet.

What do these birds look like ?

Ostrich
The world's tallest birds, ostriches are 8 ft (2.5 m)! Their loose-textured wing feathers droop. They have long, strong legs, with two large toes.

Emu
Emus are 7 ft (2.1 m) in height. Their wings are very small and are generally hidden in their long, loose feathers. They have distinctive blue patches on their necks.

Rhea
Rheas are 4 ft 2 in. (13 m) tall. They have loose wing feathers, and small feathers on their heads, faces and necks. Like Emus, rheas have three toes.

Ostriches can outrun emus and rheas over a distance.

Can ostriches, emus and rheas fly ?

No, these birds really are flightless—their wings are too small to be of any use. They are from a family called non-passerines. Greater rheas come the closest to flight when they run over grassland, they lift their wings slightly to allow some "lift" underneath which propels them along. Other flightless members of the family include southern cassowarys and brown kiwis.

Which birds can run fastest

Ostriches have very powerful legs and can run up to 40 mph (65 km/h). Emus can only travel at about 30 mph (50 km/h). In fact, emus usually prefer to walk on their long legs which are covered in scales.

Do they make good pets

No. They are easily frightened and difficult to handle. They can defend themselves by kicking. Some people believe these birds are meant to live in open plains or open deserts, semi deserts and grasslands. Ostriches are now farmed for breeding and for their meat.

What is the nesting habit of the ostrich

Female ostriches lay their eggs in shallow nests which can be 10 ft (3 m) across and are made in a hollow on the ground. They will then sit on them, to mould the nest to their bodies—and usually lay their eggs in the late afternoon! Captive female ostriches can lay up to a hundred eggs in a season. In the wild, male ostriches will find up to five extra females and mate with them.

Emus usually prefer to walk, but can reach speeds of 30 mph (50 km/h).

FACT BYTES

If you want to eat ostrich meat, it's called "volaise."

Emus are good swimmers which can live in the wild for up to thirty years.

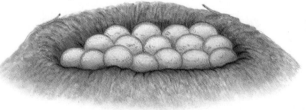

Female ostriches lay their eggs in a shallow depression on the ground.

OWLS

Most owls sleep during the day and hunt at night. They are able to fly noiselessly because of their thick plumage which allows the wind to pass over the wings.

Which owls are the rarest

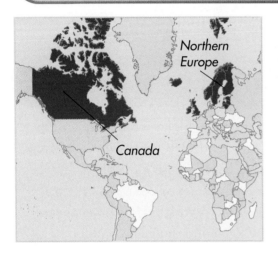

Northern Europe

Canada

Brown fish owls were known in northern Israel. They once bred in wadis (watercourses) near scrubland and trees. Said to have made strange screaming sounds, some people think they are now extinct. Many "rare" owls, such as northern hawk owls, are seen in zoos, but they are not necessarily rare in their own countries.

Which owls can be seen in Britain

Long-eared owl

Long-eared owls breed in forests. In winter, as many as twenty long eared owls may roost together.

Short-eared owl

Short-eared owls live across Europe. Unusually for an owl, they hunt during the daytime.

Barn owl

Barn owls are becoming increasingly rare and do not always nest in barns, choosing holes in trees, old ruins or, more commonly, specially sited nest boxes.

FACT BYTES

The little owl can only be seen in Europe.

A pair of snowy owls bred in the Shetland Islands, UK, in the 1960s, but the male has now gone missing so the future of "snowies" in the UK is uncertain.

Which owls are the most beautiful

Many people think snowy owls are the most attractive, due to their wide wingspans of white feathers and glowing amber eyes. The males are completely white; females have small black spots on their white feathers. Their homes are in the Arctic tundra, where their thick feathers keep them warm.

A female snowy owl.

Can owls attack people

Screech owls, with their large ear tufts, are particularly aggressive owls and will attack birds and mammals much larger than themselves if they are hungry enough. It would be wise to watch them from a distance as they are known to have attacked humans who get too close to their young. Tawny owls, which can act similarly, sometimes nest in gardens and near towns.

A tawny owl guarding its nest.

How do owls catch their prey

Owls rely on their excellent eyesight and hearing to launch surprise attacks. Many owls hunt by flying low over the ground or by watching from their perches before swooping to seize their prey. Barn owls, for example, have long powerful legs and can catch mice and rats.

A tawny owl.

BIRDS OF PREY

There are over 45 different species listed as birds of prey. They come in all sorts of different sizes and shapes but they are all meat-eaters with hooked bills and strong feet. Most birds of prey catch and kill their food.

Where are vultures found and what do they eat ?

Vultures have a reputation for watching sick animals and waiting for them to die so that they can feast on their meat. Vultures do eat flesh, but many types have a varied diet, including bone marrow, which they eat by swallowing and digesting bones. They are found in most parts of America, Africa, Asia, the Middle East, and southern Europe.

Where do eagles live ?

There are about 59 different species of eagle throughout the world, and they can be found on every continent except Antarctica. Eagles come in all different shapes and sizes. Bald eagles are magnificent birds that are only found in North America. Although they are not the largest of the eagles, they are still an impressive size. Harpy eagles of the rainforests of South America are perhaps the largest.

Vultures soaring in the air.

What are kites and where can they be found ?

Kites are slender birds of prey which look extremely graceful when flying. The easiest kites to spot are red kites, which are found in most parts of Europe, Asia, northwest Africa, and the Canary and Cape Verde islands. Primarily scavengers and opportunists, they prey on birds, small mammals, earthworms, and carrion.

A red kite.

How do these birds catch their food

Birds of prey have very sharp, curved claws called talons, with which they can crush their prey. Golden eagles are very powerful killing machines. They tend to fly very fast and low, and dives in for their prey with slanting movements. Their presence in the air must be terrifying for their victims.

A golden eagle swoops in on a hare.

Talons are sharp, curved claws.

What noises do birds of prey make

Common buzzards make highly distinctive "mewing" sounds. Red kites, meanwhile, make insistent "complaining" sounds. Turkey vultures are usually silent but will hiss or grunt when they are feeding or at nest.

FACT BYTES

Sparrowhawks not only fly over low ground to catch their prey, but have also been known to chase small birds on foot!

A buzzard sitting on a fence post.

PARROTS AND MACAWS

Parrots are beautiful and intelligent birds which form strong pair bonds. Parrots have excellent memories. There are over two hundred species of parrot in captivity and many more species flying free in the world.

Where do wild parrots live ❓

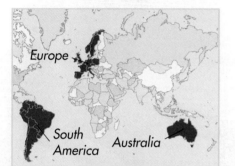

Europe

South America

Australia

Most parrots are found in tropical parts of the world but there are some types that live in cold areas, in the same places as penguins. Perhaps one of the most spectacularly colored parrots is the male red-winged parrot, which is found in Australia. The head, neck and underparts of these parrots are bright green while their lower backs are very bright blue. Red-fan parrots, distinguished by red feathers that form spectacular ruffs when they are excited, are native to forests in northern areas of South America. The Monk Parakeet, or Quaker as it is commonly known, is a native of South America and has managed to establish feral colonies around the United States. Large colonies of ring-necked parakeets have established themselves across several parts of Europe.

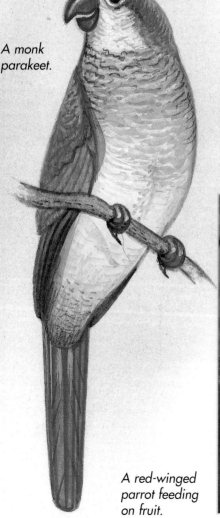

A monk parakeet.

A red-winged parrot feeding on fruit.

Are there many types of parrot ❓

There are three hundred species of parrot. Some species do not include the word parrot in their name—micans, macaws, lovebirds, and cockatoos, for example. Typical parrots are medium sized with quite short, broad tails. Parakeets are parrots with long tails.

Right: A blue and yellow macaw.

Left: A pair of lovebirds.

Are parrots intelligent ❓

Sometimes people forget that parrots are intelligent birds. If caged parrots are not getting enough attention they will make noises or fling food all over the place. Parrots need to be talked to and kept active. They can imitate your sound, so you can teach them to say a few phrases. However, that doesn't mean they understand what they are saying.

Can I understand parrot behavior ❓

If parrots stretch their wings they are feeling secure. If parrots fluff and ruffle their feathers they are telling you that they trust you. When parrots are settling down to sleep they grind their beaks. If parrots preen their tails it means that they do not see you as a threat. If you have a parrot, you really need to understand its behavior so that you can keep it happy.

Stretching wings.

Fluffing and ruffling.

Preening tail feathers.

FACT BYTES

Not all parrots are seed eaters. Some eat pollen, nectar, palm nuts, and figs.

Budgerigars were the first of the parrot family to become pets.

In R.L. Stevenson's book *Treasure Island* Long John Silver had a pet parrot.

GAME

Chickens, turkeys, and game birds are all bred to be eaten and their eggs have a multitude of culinary uses! However, not all of these birds are eaten—who would want to eat a beautiful peacock?

Are turkeys found in the wild ❓

Turkeys were once found in the wild in North America. In the 1500s they were introduced to Britain and Europe. They have been kept in captivity ever since—although escaped turkeys now breed in Germany. Wild turkeys are timid and live in forests and clearings. In the wild, they eat berries, seeds, and nuts. Wild turkeys live in flocks during cold winter months.

A common turkey.

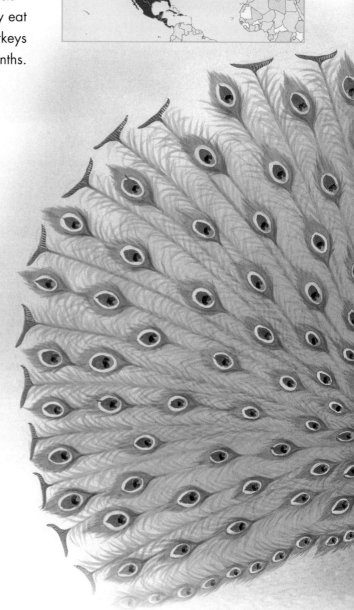

Where do pheasants come from ❓

Pheasants were first found living near the Black Sea. Although the Greeks and Romans ate them, they were not brought back to Britain until the time of the Crusades, over 700 years ago. The common pheasant can be found in Europe, North America, and Asia. Perhaps the most unusual pheasants are the gray peacocks that fan out their feathers "on display" to reveal lots of "ocelli" (eye spots).

What are pea fowls ❓

Peafowls are commonly known as peacocks. In the wild, they live in tropical forests, feeding on seeds, fruits, insects, and even mice! You will often see them on farms and in other enclosures, fanning out what looks like their tails. In fact, it is only the males that have such colorful sets of feathers which are used to attract females.

How many types of grouse are there

There are three types of grouse in Britain. Willow grouse and red grouse live in moorland areas. Red grouse keep their brown plumage all year while willow grouse have white bellies and become white in winter. Black grouse live on the edge of forests, sometimes roosting in trees. They have white, elongated tail feathers.

A willow grouse (left) and a red grouse (right).

What habitats do pheasants like

Pheasants like to live along edges of open fields, bushy hedgerows and forest edges. They often inhabit marshy areas and are rarely found in dry areas. They nest on the ground beneath thick vegetation on a sparse lining of leaves. In Europe and America they are bred on game farms and released for hunting.

A peacock showing its spectacular feather display.

FACT BYTES

In very hot weather, it is possible to fry hens' eggs on the hood of a car.

Partridges and pheasants can both fly—but are better at running!

GAME

BIRDS OF PARADISE

Birds of paradise are beautiful. They have very long, colorful tail feathers and groups of feathers on their bodies like ornamental plumes.

When were the tail feathers first used by humans ❓

Tail feathers were first traded in southeast Asia over 5,000 years ago. People in Papua New Guinea have worn the tail feathers of birds of paradise for centuries. The birds' skins were also once sold but their sale, along with that of plumes, was banned in 1922.

A bird of paradise preening its tail feathers.

A bird of paradise eating an insect.

What do birds of paradise eat ❓

Each of the 42 different species of birds of paradise have slightly different diets. Most eat nectar, insects, spiders, and fruit; some eat frogs and lizards. Sicklebills have long, down-curved bills which they use for digging insects from rotten wood or from behind bark. Rifle birds dig out insect larvae from wood.

Where can I see birds of paradise ❓

Most species of birds of paradise make their homes in New Guinea, Australia and New Zealand, so generally people are most likely to see them in captivity.

A blue bird of paradise.

New Guinea

Australia

New Zealand

What are the differences between the sexes

The males are always more brightly colored. One of the brightest are the rarely seen king birds of paradise, which hide in lowland rain forests. The males have very bright orange-to-red plumage and long tail feathers with coiled feather vanes, but the females are drab brown in color. The male lesser birds of paradise have lovely tufts of plumes on their flanks. Their plumes are white, becoming yellow near their bodies. Their faces are white with blue near their beaks.

Male and female king birds.

How do male birds of paradise attract females

Some birds of paradise puff out their plumage, raise their tail plumes and begin to scream. Sometimes, the males gather in groups on bare branches high in forests and call to the females. They then arch their plumes. Others fan out their feathers and vibrate their bodies, before making throbbing sounds, rather like machines.

FACT BYTES

In 1520, the Sultan of Batchian gave Captain Magellan a bird of paradise skin for the King of Spain.

In the 1500s, Europeans thought birds of paradise floated in heaven. They believed the birds fed on dew until they died and fell to Earth. It took almost two hundred years for Europeans to realize this was not the truth!

A bird of paradise performing a courting ritual.

BIRDS OF PARADISE

HUMMINGBIRDS

Hummingbirds are some of the most exciting birds to be found in the Americas. They can fly forwards, upwards, downwards and unlike any other birds, backwards! They get their name from the sound their wings make.

What exactly are hummingbirds

When Europeans first saw hummingbirds they thought the birds were a cross between insects and birds because they were so small! We now know that they are simply birds. Prized for their variety and color, native Americans once used hummingbird feathers for decoration and even wore hummingbird earrings. Aztec kings wore cloaks made from hummingbird skins.

How do hummingbirds hum

The rapid beating of their wings makes a humming noise. Hummingbirds are small, but generally the bigger the birds, the louder the hums. Broad-tailed hummingbirds are thought to have the loudest hums—even though they are not quite the biggest hummingbirds.

A hummingbird beats its wings so rapidly it creates a hum.

How many species of hummingbird are there

Canada

USA

Costa Rica

Jamaica

South America

There are over three hundred species—all of different colors. They are found in the USA, Canada, South America, Costa Rica, and Jamaica.

FACT BYTES

It was once thought that hummingbirds migrated on the backs of swans and geese.

Which are the biggest and smallest hummingbirds

A hummingbird extracting nectar using its long bill.

The largest are the giant hummingbirds of South America. They weigh 0.05 lb (20 g). The smallest are blue hummingbirds which weigh 0.004 lb (2.2 g). The longest are the blue throats. Calliope hummingbirds, at just 3 in. (8 cm) in length, are North America's smallest birds. They are often found by streams in conifer forests.

A giant hummingbird.

A blue hummingbird.

What do hummingbirds eat

They use their long bills to eat nectar. Pet hummingbirds need to eat mixtures of heated sugar and water. The sugar and water solutions are cooled before they are eaten.

What other hummingbirds are there

Strangely-named booted racquet-tails are hummingbirds. They get their name from the males, which have long tails that end in small, rounded feathers. The birds themselves use their fast and bee-like flying ability to dart and weave in and out of foliage. Their hums sound deep as their little wings beat fast. Red-tailed comets are also hummingbirds. They have green heads, red bodies and long, forked red tails—although the tips of their tails are black. Red-tailed comets fan their tails and wave them up and down when perched.

SUNBIRDS AND HONEYCREEPERS

The dazzling sunbirds of Africa, Asia, and Australia are among the most glamorous of all birds. Honeycreepers are found in South America, Trinidad, and Tobago, while Hawaiian honeycreepers live exclusively in Hawaii. Both sunbirds and honeycreepers live on insects, fruit and nectar, which they suck from flowers with their long, curved bills.

What do sunbirds look like ?

Sunbirds have vivid green colors.

Sunbirds have brilliant, colorful, glossy, shimmering feathers. They look like hummingbirds but have strong feet and legs and short, rounded wings. They have long bills for collecting insects and their tube-like tongue allows them to suck-up nectar easily. Some have long tails that are almost half their body's length. They are 3-12 in. (9-30 cm) long and weigh 0.01-0.04 lb (5-20 g).

For what do honeycreepers use their bills ?

Honeycreepers are small, colorful birds with a great variety of remarkably shaped bills. These are adapted to different feeding habits: from powerful bills that can crack seeds to very thin bills that taper downwards. In one species, the bills take up one-third of the birds' entire length.

Where do they live ?

Honeycreepers are found in forests or woody areas. Hawaiian honeycreepers live in forests on the sides of volcanoes, at heights of up to 9,900 ft (3,000 m), as their original habitats lower down have been destroyed over the years by agriculture and development. Most sunbirds are also forest birds, but some, like Palestine sunbirds, occur in patches of vegetation in deserts.

What are their eating habits

Sunbirds spend about twenty percent of their time foraging for food—mainly nectar—although they may snack on the occasional insect. Rather than traveling far for their dinner, they will often choose territories and wait for the flowers growing there to become plump with nectar. They may "steal" the nectar by piercing through the base of the flower rather than going through the top. Honeycreepers, by contrast, spend almost half their time foraging for food (they spend the other half resting to recover). Most eat fruit as well as nectar, and one species, the purple honeycreeper is very partial to bananas.

A honeycreeper eating a banana.

How do they build their nests

Sunbird nests are unusual. They are pear-shaped or oval, made of grass, fibers and cobwebs, and are suspended from the ends of twigs. They usually nest low in bushes and trees but also close to humans—olive-backed sunbirds in Malaysia have nested in balconies, porches, and corridors! Honeycreepers nest in tree canopies, tree cavities, rock cavities, and grass tussocks.

How common are sunbirds and honeycreepers

There are estimated to be about 120 species of sunbird but only about 23 species of Hawaiian honeycreeper, half of which are endangered. This is due to disease spread by mosquitoes which arrived in the 1820s on whaling ships. More species of native birds have become extinct in Hawaii in the last two hundred years than anywhere else on the planet.

Hawaiian honeycreeper perching on a branch.

FACT BYTES

The bright red feathers of 'I'iwi-Hawaiian honeycreepers were highly prized by the Hawaiians who used them to make feathered capes and helmets for their chiefs.

One of the smallest sunbirds in the Sungei Buloh Nature Park in Singapore is the crimson sunbird. Adult males weigh only 0.01 lb (7 g) and appear like tiny red dots among the vegetation.

GLOSSARY

Adapted
Changed to suit their surroundings.

Air sacs
Sacs full of air so that the birds can breathe in water.

Alaudidae
Family of birds that includes the lark.

Aphids
Small insects, such as greenfly.

Buoyancy
Ability to keep afloat.

Carrion
Dead and rotting flesh.

Chattering
High pitched noises that sound like speech.

Common Jay
Type of crow which steals eggs.

Coucal
Type of cuckoo, born with coarse hair.

Crevices
Gaps in walls.

Crow
A large, mainly black, bird with a harsh call, of Europe and Asia.

Cuckoo
Any bird of the family *Cuculida*, having pointed wings and a long tail.

Dipper
Any of a genus of aquatic songbirds that inhabit fast-flowing streams.

Egg
The oval, or round, reproductive body laid by the females of some animals, consisting of a developing embryo, its food store and often jelly, all surrounded by an outer shell or membrane.

Egret
Any of various wading birds similar to herons but usually having white plumage, and in the breeding season, long feathery plumes.

Emerald dove
Australian bird that only flies when in danger.

Eurasia
The continents of Europe and Asia considered as a whole.

Feral
Species, or individual, that were once domesticated but have been released or escaped and have become wild.

Fledges
Ready to fly.

Genus
A class of objects, or individuals, that can be divided into two or more groups or species.

Gull
An aquatic bird such as the common gull having long pointed wings, short legs, and a mostly white plumage.

Heron
Any of various wading birds having a long neck, slim body, and a plumage that is commonly gray or white.

Honey creeper
A small tropical American songbird having a slender downward-curving bill and feeding on nectar.

Hovering
Staying motionless in the air.

Ibis
Any of various wading birds that occur in warm regions and have a long thin down-curved bill.

Incubation
Supply of heat to eggs to keep them warm.

Killdeer
A North American plover.

Lapwing
Type of wader with shimmering green plumage and a black crest.

Lark
Any brown bird of a predominantly Old World family of songbirds.

Larvae
An early form of a creature that changes into something else.

Magpie
Type of crow with a reputation as a thief.

Mane
Long hair that grows from the neck.

Manx shearwater
Type of gull that glides, or "shears" over the water as it follows a boat.

Migrant
A bird that moves from one area of the world to another.

Motacillidae
Family of birds that includes wagtails and pipits.

Nectar
Sugary fluid produced in flowers.

New World
The Americas; the western hemisphere.

Northern waterthrush
Type of warbler that searches through dead foliage for food.

Old World
That part of the world that was known before the discovery of the Americas.

Ostrich
A fast-running flightless African bird that is the largest living bird.

Ovenbird
Another type of warbler that searches through dead foliage for food.

Parasitic
Living off others.

Passerine
Of, relating to, or belonging to an order of birds characterized by the perching habit.

Peacock
A male peafowl, having a crested head and very large tail marked with blue and green eyelike spots.

Peafowl
Either of two large pheasants of India and Ceylon and of south-east Asia.

Pesticides
Chemicals used to kill pests.

Phasianidae
Bird family that includes the peafowl and peacock.

Pied
Markings of two or more colors.

Pigeon
Any of numerous related birds having a heavy body; small head, short legs, and long pointed wings.

Pipit
Any of various songbirds, having brownish speckled plumage and a long tail.

Plover
Any of a family of shore birds, typically having a round head, straight bill and large pointed wings.

Plumage
The feathery part of a bird.

Pollen
Food produced from plants.

Red kite
Bird of prey found in some parts of Britain.

Rock Dove
Ancestor of the tame pigeon, this bird still exists in the wild.

Ruffles
Erected (standing up on top of head) feathers.

Sheen
Gleaming brightness.

Sickle-shaped
Crescent shaped.

Spoonbill
Closest British relative to the ibis.

Swallow
Any of various songbirds having long pointed wings, a forked tail, short legs, and a rapid flight.

Swift
Any of various insectivorous birds of the Old World. They spend most of their time on the wing.

Volaise
The name given to ostrich meat.

Vulture
Bird of prey that eats carrion.

Wagtail
Any of various passerine songbirds of Eurasia and Africa, having a very long tail that wags when the bird walks.

Warbler
A small, active songbird of the Old World.

Wingbeat
A complete cycle of movement of the wing by a bird in flight.

Woodpecker
Brightly colored climbing bird.

GLOSSARY

INDEX

Acknowledgements
Key:Top—t; middle—m; bottom—b; left—l; right—r;
3: Top That!.4: (t,m)Corel; (b) M.Hunt/RSPB Images. 8: Mike Lane/RSPB Images. 11: Mike McKavett/RSPB Images. 13: Mark Hamblin/RSPB Images. 15: (m) Gordon Langsbury/RSPB Images;(b) Mark Hamblin/RSPB Images. 19: Eric Hosking/Corbis. 20: David Hosking/Corbis. 21: Chris Gomersall/RSPB Images. 23: Corel. 25: (t) David Hosking/ Corbis; (m) Topham picture point. 26: Darrell Gulin/Corbis. 27: Laurie Campbell/RSPB Images. 28: Andy Hay/RSPB Images. 31: BYB/Rex Features. 33: Niall Benvie/RSPB Images. 34: Mike Read/RSPB Images.36: Corel. 37: Dave Watts/NHPA. 39: John Cancalosi/Naturepl. 40: Corel.